# THE BAMBOO WIFE

# THE BAMBOO WIFE
by Leona Sevick

TRIO
HOUSE
PRESS

Sevick, Leona
1st edition

ISBN: 978-1-949487-29-9
Library of Congress Control Number: 2023946807

Interior design by Natasha Kane
Cover design by Joel Coggins
Editing by Natasha Kane and Ali Shafer

Trio House Press, Inc.
Minneapolis
www.triohousepress.org

*I am no bird; and no net ensnares me.*
– Charlotte Brontë, *Jane Eyre*

for Adah Jane, my rover

# TABLE OF CONTENTS

## I

Hapa / 3

Sometimes they come back to me in dreams / 5

Stone Grandfather / 6

The Bamboo Wife / 7

Korean Wedding Ducks / 8

Sokcho, South Korea / 9

The rest of what was there / 10

Elegy for Farmer Pak / 11

I stop somewhere waiting for you / 13

Blind / 14

The Noctambulist / 15

The Heifer / 16

My Father's Lessons / 18

Curfew / 20

Guarding George Wallace / 21

Pedal / 22

Spondylosis / 23

## II

Doll's House, Provincetown Museum / 29

This for That / 30

Ivy in the House / 31

Sun and Moon / 32

Scorpling / 33

Ride Along / 35

Sting / 36

Doubles / 37

Resurrection / 38

Dilettante / 40

Choosy Females, Profligate Males / 42

Your turn / 43

Reckless / 44

Sleeper / 45

Kraken / 46

Je mange mes mots / 47

Dirt Move / 49

Stranger Things / 50

## III

End of Days / 55

Menagerie of Broken Things / 56

Copulatory Embrace / 57

Cooper's Rules / 58

Drink Ghazal / 60

Fallout / 61

My Vampyre / 62

The Lost Boys, 1987 / 63

Familiar / 64

Confession / 66

The Shopping / 67

Thigmotaxis / 69

Mutualism / 70

Steady, Girl / 71

Collateral / 72

Wreck and Ruin / 73

Retold / 74

Run / 76

**IV**

Untenable / 81

Pilgrim / 82

Virginia is for Lovers / 83

Homecoming / 85

Welcome Home / 86

Hemlock / 87

Ghost Trees / 89

That House / 90

The House Speaks / 91

Land of the Lotus Eaters / 92

Johns Hopkins Hospital at the Corner of Orleans and
N. Broadway / 93

Something / 94

The Trees / 95

My Mother's Kitchen / 96

Third Sunday / 97

Once, I Thought He Knew Everything / 98

Inherited / 99

Filial / 100

Grief Cat / 102

Big Pipe Creek / 103

Notes / 107

Acknowledgments / 109

Gratitude / 113

About the Author / 115

**I**

## Hapa

Taking my order by phone, she asks me
*What do you look like? So I can find you?*

Except that's not how she says it. Dropping
words the way my Korean mother did,

still making herself understood, this girl
waits while I decide. Pausing, as I do,

as I've done since the first time someone asked
me with genuine interest *What are you?*

I answer this woman in a way I
already know she will never accept,

take the chance I never take. *Yes*, she says,
*I think I know you.* Spotting her just as

she comes through the door, I wait for her to
scan the room, find me, then decide. She

approaches, tosses bags on the table,
mouths the word I know she's thinking, the word

I've heard a dozen times. *Hapa.* It is
the one my mother hated, the reason

I was grown before she took me home to
meet her people. I see her stiff face, black

eyes of resentment at their turned backs, their
conditional love. Now I speak the truth

of who I am, or at least half of who
I am. I give this judgmental girl a

broad smile. I thank her, watch her go, knowing half a truth is better than any lie.

## Sometimes they come back to me in dreams

It's two in the morning and she startles
awake, thinking it's the dog or her son's
voice. An almost remembered word works her
tongue, and she wants to recall it herself.
She slows her breath and listens closely, hears
the soft chatter of women speaking fast
and low. They talk factories, ungrateful
children, whisper the ugly words they hear
from strangers. They bicker over ways to
cook rice noodles. Beneath blankets sown by
hand with a thousand tiny stitches, she
feels them combing her hair with rough fingers.
Finally, she recalls the word. *Hoon-jah*. Alone.

## Stone Grandfather

(*Dol Hareubang*, Jeju Island, South Korea)

And there you sit, your basalt belly swollen heavy,
a gentle smile playing at your stone lips. To say I
sought you out would be a bald-faced lie, but I will
admit that seeing you standing there all alone on
Hyeopjae Beach, the long tide pulling at the sand around
you, gave me pause. Towering ominous and amused,
your bulging eyes the diameter of cymbals,
you wait patiently for me to speak, an outdoor
priest in his open-air confessional. Beckoning
with giant fingers, you intimate I should kneel
at the idea of your feet. *Tell me your troubles.*

When I was a child, my grandmother, *halmoni*, urged
me to pray to *harabeogi*, ask the grandfather
for his forgiveness for every sin my child's heart
harbored. (I've since forgiven her this small cruelty.)

In this strange place, newlyweds buy their own *hareubangs*,
mock-believe you'll ensure fertility in their bright
futures. Trust me when I say that's not what I'm after.
I've had, in fact, lifetimes of that.

What I need can't be found in travel brochures, or on
the strangely-worded plaques that appear with you on this
honeymoon island. I need the old beliefs, the ones
the fishermen and sailors clung to years ago. No
matter what they had done or who they had injured, you
looked at them with eyes that said beloved, said *you are
worthy of my love, of others' love. I can see you.*

## The Bamboo Wife

If one bright day you find yourself moving through
the rooms of the Jeju folklore museum,

you might pause at the domestic exhibits,
wonder at the strange, closed basket as wide as

a drum and as long as a yardstick. They call
it "bamboo wife," and carefully printed signs

tell you that in warmer months, men would wrap their
arms and legs around her cage-body to sleep,

her ribs free from flesh, the air moving through her
to cool the sleeper. Perhaps you think this a

strange marriage: the wife stiff and silent, her spouse
breathing into her his stale, sour air, arms

locked in a tight embrace around nothing. Where
has she gone, living wife? Out to the paddy

field in search of a soft breeze, the cold water
cupping her feet as she reaches for the sky.

## Korean Wedding Ducks

Once you have chosen a wife,
find the man who will carve your

ducks. He will have many sons
and gold hidden in satin

bags that only he can find.
This man must be clean, he must

be free from illness and have
a good wife. When you find him,

ask him to carve you two ducks,
one whose bill is wider than

the other's. He must bury
his knife deep in the ground, must,

when he's finished, refuse all
requests. Give these lovely dark

ducks to your soon-to-be wife,
When you see one duck turned from

the other, know for certain
you have failed her again.

## Sokcho, South Korea

Five and a half hours in the back of a rented van
with the people you love most (now least) in this
world will make you embrace almost any city,
even one just north of the 38th parallel, thirty miles
from North Korea. Looking out at those cerulean
waters, at families sprawled on towels under
a rainbow of umbrellas, it's hard to imagine the lives
of people who breathe on the other side of the trawling
lines. I step closer to the water's edge, feel the cramps
in my legs give way. I watch fishermen who leave
these harbors never knowing they'll return. I suppose
you get used to it, concede you might misjudge
the distance out, that the fast boat approaching your
starboard isn't friendly. Do those men kiss their wives
longer in the morning? Linger at the bedroom doors
of their children? Or are they like the rest of us, stacking
our chips on the color we always choose. I turn back
to the van, hold my tongue and slide open the door.

## The rest of what was there

It was only a second's view of her breasts,
so small you could have cupped them both in the palm
of one of your hands. Our mother ran toward her
with a towel to shield from view what the waves had
done, stripped her of the bikini top now lying
at the bottom of the ocean. We loved this
girl who climbed onto a plane and sat still as
stones for the endless flight to America.
In her luggage we found colored pencils and
charcoal wrapped in handkerchiefs, large sheets of sketch
pads ripped from their books and folded into small
squares. We called her *Ee-mo*, Auntie, and
between her shifts waiting tables at the bar,
she would draw us anything we asked. Fancy
women, their white skin outlined in blackest ink,
their eyes so large and round they eclipsed the rest
of what was there. Her hair was still blue-black at fifty.
After the diagnosis and surgery, when her breasts had
been handled and marked, then scalpeled off,
her hair turned a whisper white. I wondered
if she saw herself the way I still see her—
brown and blazing glorious in the noonday sun.

## Elegy for Farmer Pak

Though I'd driven by his farm perhaps a hundred times,
the farm that used to be my grandfather's, I never

remember seeing Mr. Pak standing erect. His wide
straw hat tilted over his bent form, he'd push his sun

stained hands into the earth, grabbing weed roots, fingering
garlic bulbs into place by instinct, a primal knowledge.

Just below his brim, I could see the dark rich
color of his face, creased and thin, *an old face*, my mother

said, though he was two decades younger than she.
His son once told me that seven generations of

Korean farmers had taught him to use the simplest tools,
and the boy, whose English was a lifeboat of words

for his family, offered this fact defensively, as if I
who once offered my own mother the same lifeboat

might stand in judgment. I'm sorry I never
told the son how much I'd admired his father, that

I stood in awe of the way he coaxed strangely shaped
peppers out of the unforgiving clay, dried them on

blankets in the noonday sun, how he took the time
to frame the borders of his vegetable gardens

with *mugunghwa*, the pink rose bushes that reminded
him and my mother of home. Before he died, he'd bring

basket after basket of squash to my family—
his language of respect and gratefulness. Seeing him

at work, I sometimes thought of the rich white men
who owned this land, whose slaves worked

the red earth three long centuries before he did.
I think of his silent greeting of the sun's strong pull on days

when God willed it, his acceptance of the rains
when the deep cracks in the blood-red clay called out with desire.

## I stop somewhere waiting for you

Gravel crunching under tires, the big engine of the Crown Vic strains against the low gear as he inches up behind her. Turning, she spots first the blue and red lights on the top of the car, hears the slamming door and the creaking belt and holster. How frightened she is, wondering what she's doing wrong, what code she's breaking in this crazy country where rules are printed in straight, sharp lines she cannot read or write. His face, rigid and red with what she takes for anger, tells her she shouldn't be walking alone on this country road, a stranger in a town of white faces, hers the first blue-black head and lidless eyes they've ever seen. Taking long strides toward her, he says something she cannot hear at first, so he repeats it loudly a second time. *Urdee manura hang-gook sahdom e-eh-yoh.* "My wife is Korean." She nods yes, and his face relaxes as he stammers out more syllables he'd learned in Inchon when he was a soldier. This is the woman we call Auntie. She comes to our house every Saturday night to play *hah-toh* with our mother, the plastic cards slapping together on the hand-sewn blanket they crouch on as they play, knees drawn up around their elbows, their laughter stretching and contracting into the night. This is how he saves her. This is how he saves himself, too.

## Blind

Once, my brother and I thought she was just
a terrible driver. Too many times to count,

she'd steer us home from town in darkness,
headlights turned off, the streetlamps scarce

and anyway not reaching as far as we needed
them to. She drove slowly enough, her hands

at 9 and 3 like they used to teach us. Our road,
twisted and narrow, was darker still, and when

one of us would shout *Turn on your headlights!*
she'd pause, reach for the knob slowly, shake her

head as we howled. Did she choose not to see
the factory where she worked, the chipped paint

houses, the cars on cinder blocks lining
the road? Maybe she forgot on purpose.

## The Noctambulist

What dreams will make a child
rise from sleep and circle
a cold, dark house at two
in the morning? It took less than
a minute for my father to waken,
run from his bedroom to
the living room to switch off
the eight-track belting Marvin Gaye
at full blast. One by one, he'd
click off the lights I'd flicked
on, move to the kitchen where
I'd set the stand mixer on high,
left the toaster warming phantom
bread. I picture my father
groggy from the sleeplessness
my wandering instilled.
When all was unplugged,
he'd stumble back to the room
where I sat on the sofa,
staring at nothing. Gently he
ushered me back to my bed, heeding
the old words *don't wake a walker*.
What I wouldn't give to return
to those strange nights in my father's
house, to silence defeated by
brightness and vibration, to trade
these to-do lists and schedules,
the mounting bills, these pulsing
anxieties that waken me at two
in the morning, to begin again.

## The Heifer

Sometimes I think about the cows and how he
really loved them. Every post hole dug by hand,

the long, smooth boards nailed up perfectly. How he
spent hours painting the fence black with creosote

and oil, his rough hands and face flecked and burning.
Winter mornings he mended gates, poured corn feed

into troughs, pitched hay onto frozen grass while
watching froth form along their steaming, swollen

lips. I thought she must be dead the morning he
went looking for the heifer. Running back to the

house, shouting for blankets, for a bucket, he
called Doctor Mathews and then grabbed the handsaw.

At some distance I followed him, afraid of
what I'd find when I reached them. Kneeling by her

head, her gray tongue lolling and still, my father
sawed quickly through the low fencing that trapped her

head when she was nibbling grass under the boards.
She must have pulled and struggled for hours. Her eyes

jumping in their sockets, big as golf balls, he
talked softly, stroked the coarse red fur on her neck

and waited for the vet. My father nursed her
through the night, and at daybreak the rifle shot

woke me. By the time I returned from school, her
body was gone; he never spoke of her again.

I learned from him that suffering can spoil meat,
that gentleness will confound a brutal man.

## My Father's Lessons

If I told you I climbed into an old car
with an ex-con and a philandering drunk,
neither of whom I'd met before,
you'd shake your head long and slow.

With an ex-con and a philandering drunk?
You'd say you're just asking for trouble,
you'd shake your head long and slow.
Did I tell you they were famous writers?

You'd say you're just asking for trouble.
They probably invited you along—
(did I tell you they were famous writers?)
because at 46 you still look pretty good.

They probably invited you along—
you'd say I'm not at all surprised—
because at 46 you still look pretty good,
and who doesn't want to be admired?

You'd say I'm not at all surprised,
because let's face it you're never surprised.
And who doesn't want to be admired?
If I told you we spent the whole night—

because let's face it you're never surprised—
drinking whiskey and laughing.
If I told you we spent the whole night
and that old man wobbly-walked me

drinking whiskey and laughing
to my door, said goodnight
and that old man wobbly-walked me
and kissed me chastely on the mouth.

To my door, said goodnight.
You'd say I was lucky. Did you hear?
and kissed me chastely on the mouth.
If I told you this isn't the first time

you'd say I was lucky. Did you hear?
I've made bad decisions and lived.
If I told you this isn't the first time
I've lived to not regret it.

I've made bad decisions and lived;
[neither of whom I'd met before!]
I've lived to not regret it.
If I told you I climbed into an old car...

## Curfew

We knew that stretch of road by heart,
could have driven it blindfolded, almost.
So we flew, blue lights from the dashboard
recalling scenes from *The Empire Strikes Back*.
I knew we'd hit 80 when the truck started shaking.
My brother stared straight ahead, told me
silently that one word from me and he'd kill
the dash lights. We'd be rumble-flying
through the dark. All those times we pushed
and punched each other, all the hard words
we couldn't take back, the times our mother
chose him over me meant nothing to me now.
By the time our front wheels hit the driveway
he'd started breathing again, his stomach muscles
tortured from holding his breath. 10:58. We'd
made it, slipping through the door just as our
father was switching off the tv in the living room.

## Guarding George Wallace

One May day in nineteen seventy-two
Arthur Bremer shot Wallace five times,
a bullet lodging in his spine in
such a way he'd never walk again.
We know that Bremer was crazy, not
a martyr for good. Here is madness
where we crave reason, bald desire for
fame where we'd prefer conviction. My
father, twenty-five and gentle still,
stood with his straight back to the door
of Wallace's hospital room, gun at
his hip and shoes polished to a high
shine. He would have laid down his life
for an unworthy man. Who among us
chooses who we care for, who we serve?
I have forgiven him nearly everything.

## Pedal

The gravel path is steep—a two-mile slog straight
up the mountain, no switchbacks to ease the climb.

Riding my daughter's bike, the good one her dad
bought her and she doesn't use, I push past camps

littered with bottles and cans, cars whose owners
are nowhere to be found. Losing myself in

the sound of my breathing, I click through chainrings
and gears, try to shift smoothly. I scan the road

for potholes, for rocks, pray my brakes will hold on
the other side. Stomping uphill on the bike,

my heart thumping hard in my chest and in my
ears, I still hear his voice when trouble finds me.

Suddenly I'm ten again, straining against
the slope, his shouts pushing me uphill: *Pedal.*

## Spondylosis

is the word she uses, our faces
pressed close to the screen, our
knees nearly touching as we stare
at the shadows marking my spine,
the thinning spaces between my
neck bones. Speaking softly, her
long index finger gently tracing
the tiny sunbursts pinned to my
vertebrae, the word emerges from
her lips in lovely lilting syllables,
offers answers, hope for relief.
*Old trauma*, she says—a diagnosis
I know is right, hard years stacking
on years until bones pinch threaded
nerves and I am here, stiff with pain.
*Let's see what we can do about this.*
When we were young, my brother
would hold my head just under
the jaw bones, offer traction while
I sat cross-legged on the floor.
He'd do this for hours, balance
skinny arms on knees while we
watched tv, shake out his limbs
during commercials. Most days
he was like any other big brother,
cruel and loud, teasing and selfish,
but on the bad days, when lamps
crashed to the floor, when we had
breakfast for dinner and the silence
between our parents was wide as
sinkholes, he could be as gentle
as this woman I hardly know.
Cradling my head with strong
hands, she lightly pulls and turns
it this way and that, watches my

face closely for signs of pain.
When a tear crawls down my cheek,
she does not ask me if she should
stop. Instead, she presses down on
each shoulder, says *let it go*.

# II

## Doll's House, Provincetown Museum

Walk through the giant open jaws of the blue whale,
back toward the stunned faces of the porcelain
dolls wearing Victorian clothes and clutching real leather
purses to find the house that's the size of a small gas
stove. Set on a three-foot platform so you can peer into
its windows, point at its tiny fixtures and the books
with real and separate pages, this house glows with
a softened light that draws us closer. Pressing a cheek
against the wooden siding, your nose to the windows,
you'll discover thick plastic panels shielding its orifices
and rebuffing our fingers, the pincers and pads that long
to probe everything—the hurricane lamp half the size
of a pinky, the lovingly quilted coverlet, the perfectly
placed cup and saucer no one uses anymore. What
dreadful thing has happened to this family? Some hard
truth erupting among them on an otherwise quiet
evening, driving them out, inviting the transparent
barrier that makes it impossible to return.

## This for That

I put up with all of it. Mass every
Sunday with Father Miguel who speaks no
Spanish, the judgy parish councilmen
in their sartorial bests, *Humanae
Vitae*. I ignore the crazy pro-life
crowd, holding up grizzly pictures of dead
fetuses on street corners. I accept
the sacraments, reconciliation
that never feels like absolution, the
report that nixed contraception (despite
Vatican II), everything John Paul
ever wrote or said, Adam's rib, Isaac's
trust, and even the diddling priests and their
bastard bishops just so I can sit with my
teenaged boy and girl who will for one
hour let me quietly hold their still hands.

## Ivy in the House

In unison, my teenaged children shout "Don't!"
and so I have no choice but to leave it be—
the ivy growing up between the floorboards
in my kitchen. Yesterday I noticed its
twisting stem, its smooth green leaf unfurling by
the garbage can and wondered why no one had
plucked it. This house, its cracked chinking and tilted
doorframes, invited our emerald guest.
Though they offer no explanation, I'm sure
my boy and girl see its chief charm: resistance
to my tidying jags, my need for order
everywhere. And who can blame them? They're on
its side, this wild, bright thing unwilling to be
mastered, refusing to submit to the world.

## Sun and Moon

If you ask me anything about him,
and I mean the simplest question
about his age or what he likes to do,
I'm likely to answer in a complicated
way you are not prepared for. You
will judge me, and I will loathe you,
and we will not be friends. In earshot
of the man who shares my bed,
who cooks me scrambled eggs
in the dark hours of the morning,
I'll hold my tongue, but to you I speak
the truth of my constrained heart.
He is the love of my life, my alpha
and omega, the dark pull that began
at the blood-wash moment of his birth.
His happiness is my relief, his sadness
my undoing. And yes, if you must know,
I'm having trouble letting go, though I
won't answer for it to you or anyone.
Ask the sun and moon, who know
exactly what I mean.

## Scorpling

She caught you just
as you emerged
from her operculum,
elevating abdomen,
arranging legs.

Gently she placed you
on her back,
watched over
your fragile body
with twelve sets of eyes,
held her breath
in book lungs as you
molted and hardened.

On the days you'd climb down,
explore until hungering
brought you back to her,
she lost sight of herself,
regretted night cravings
for solitude.
You returned
until the day you didn't.

Your name is rooted in the words *to cut*.

Did your mother's mad
loving, that venom,
make you stronger
than you would have been
otherwise?

Boy, I've told you:
how we begin
is not always
how we end.

## Ride Along

Before you were born, before I carried your
boy body in the loam-scented liquid,
before I consented to your father's wish,
before I abandoned my own oft-stated wish
to be a mother to no one (or if to
someone then to dogs), before I embarked on
my own journey to become someone else,
I knew exactly who I didn't want you
to be. And now here we are: you balanced on
the lip of manhood, I objecting without
a word. *It's just a police ride along* you
say, *a project for school*, and I nod, swallow
words as fast as they come to me: *don't become
my father*. Once you rode on my rounded hip
as I erected waist-high bars to keep you
in. Now you study me with blue eyes I look
up to meet, braced for the impact of your words.
A scorpling clings to the back of its mother,
hardens and then lets her go.

## Sting

The wasps are dying in my son's
bedroom, and each morning I rush
to collect them before he wakes
and finds them on the floor. On my
knees, cheek pressed to the thin woolen
rug so I can see them at eye
level, I pick them up by their
wings, by a crooked leg, pinching
their parts like a jeweler. At first
the numbers startle me—I find
forty, then fifty striped bodies,
some twisting in hunger's throes. Soon
there are less than a dozen. Drones
who can't feed themselves rely on
their sisters, the queen's will for food.
Once my boy leaves for school, his last
year before college, I return
to the room, lay my head against
a wall, listen for their humming

## Doubles

He thinks I'm lying, denying with my silence
that this dark-haired boy, Jason, is mine. Slight, black
eyes tilted at the ends, he's my spitting image.
*He yours?* the old man asks, not unkindly, because
I've been softly cheering for this boy, twisting each
ring on my fingers and willing him with pacing
to do better, to follow through on his ground strokes
so there won't be hell to pay later. The man,
eyeing me closely, mistakes me for the loving,
devoted mother of this boy, small for sixteen.
He waits two beats before walking away. I
don't stop him, don't say *no, my boy is his partner*,
a giant with shoulders as broad as a man's. He's
the one stomping up and down the court, shouting at
Jason, pretend-cracking his racket
over his own knees every time he misses a
shot, or Jason does. I know just how my
not-son feels—that the world was made for other boys,
the ones who laugh too loudly, who expect
to be first, who get what they want, who win. I thought
it was a saying that you want the ground to swallow
you. I picture giant dirt lips opening toward me,
saving all the Jasons and me, too.

## Resurrection

My doctor's steady voice is still in my
ears, and relieved, I move along counters,

wanting to touch every crisp package,
finger the bright yellow and green ribbons,

breathe in the hazelnut rabbits, peanut
butter eggs, lift and hold them to my nose.

The Mennonite girl at the register
is watching me politely, and I don't

want to trouble her, a sweet look on her
clean face. After a while I choose two milk

chocolate bunnies, both hands full of bright
candy eggs, two brightly colored suckers

in the shape of cartoon chicks. She smiles at
me, says she likes when people take their time.

Years ago, when my boy was three, I made
his Easter basket weeks in advance, with books

and treats I'd chosen carefully then sealed
inside a blue cellophane barrier—

protection against the world. I was sure
his sister, due at the end of that month,

would kill me. When she didn't, we tore through
the plastic together, his greedy, plump

hands delighted by the things they touched. Here,
now, I want to rip apart these wrappings,

muscle through the knotted ribbons, stuff all
I can into my mouth. Reach in and in.

## Dilettante

It's really not that bad. The dark,
this walk home longer than you
want it to be, your fingers folded
into pockets where they fight
November cold, where they hide
from the moon's sharp, slivered eye.
Whatever you've been up to,
whatever kept you at the office
so late doesn't matter now.
That sound coming from over
the ridge is the pop of aluminum
against a hard leather ball, and it
takes you back to a time when
all you wanted was to sit your
ass on the cold, metal bleachers
and watch your boy play baseball.
How you loved everything about it
because he loved everything about it,
even in that hopeless season when
they were 0 for 7 and fall ball
stretched its stiff neck into winter.
You propped elbows on knees
and chin on hands for so long
you couldn't feel anything, anymore.
Lips thin with concentration, frame
vibrating with potential, your boy
stepped up to the plate and pawed
the dirt like a pony, held the ump
like a pro. You held your breath,
felt your thumping heart say
*good eye, good eye*. No matter what
happened next, the sun would come up,
as it did, tomorrow. You'll pay
your bills, throw a load into
the washer, settle into your life

pretending those pointe shoes,
that sonata wouldn't have led to
anything, anyway. Aimed toward
home and a sink full of dishes,
you bend to the wind, walk on.

## Choosy Females, Profligate Males

White coat scientists say women are choosy,
document early investments in raising

our young, tell us it's why we discriminate
among so many options while males do not.

They tell us if we make the wrong choices, we
are at far greater risk than males. No kidding.

It is true we carry them for months on end,
that every choice we make they have a share in.

Too many among us suckle them for years,
longer than we're willing to admit, invite

them into our beds, let them order our days
by their needs and desires. There's no end to what

they take from us: the energy, sound sleep, sound
mind, the limitless potential of fertile

years. You think I'm talking about offspring, here?
You ask, indignant, what of the men who spend

hours throwing every kind of ball? Who kiss
their kids each day without fail and tell them they

love them? Even these males can be profligate,
too. It's impossible to argue with science.

**Your turn**

When my brother was seven, he burned the back of his left hand on the hot coils of an old refrigerator during a game of hide and seek. It happened at the dingy home of my mother's sad friend, a woman we all called horse face. The two-inch scar, raised and ugly, nearly caused my parents' split. From time to time I caught my father looking at that scar and wondered at the resentments he harbored, the anguish of picturing the precise moment that ruined his perfect boy. Yesterday, pushing her face toward mine with a grin as wide as a bowl, my daughter showed me a chipped tooth. By the way I sucked my breath and grabbed her arm, you would have thought it was, instead, her pink tongue lying at the bottom of the chlorinated pool.

## Reckless

Every fight begins this way:
"You've handed her the gun,
the one she'll shoot me with."
And by you I mean me. And by
her I mean my teenager who'll
use whatever I leave lying around
to hurt me with. And by the gun
I mean the words. In the news
a six-year-old shoots his first-grade
teacher. A toddler waves a gun
in the hallway of an apartment
building while neighbors peer
through the judas hole to see
the world grotesque, fish-eyed.
They say *look what happens*
*when parents are just no good.*
I've learned there are a hundred
ways to be reckless with love.
I've handed her my gun—
sighted, cleaned, and loaded.
There's one in the chamber
already. And by the chamber
you know I mean my heart.

## Sleeper

The wind whips tiny blossoms off the Japanese
cherry trees, swirling them around the stiff, seated
Buddha in my garden. At this moment he seems
more alive than she is, though his pocked stone skin is
drained of color and his eyes are sealed tight against
the clean light of morning. Inside a darkened room
she sleeps, her soft, oily face unguarded, tender
frame loosely coiled. This is my girl, the one who breaks
every curfew, whose whims fly across her face in
technicolor clarity, who would rather talk
than read, who sleeps to recharge for the next excess.
When she was a toddler, I called for her, found her in
the great room where she'd climbed outside the staircase to
the second story, held onto wooden spindles,
her sticky toes inching along the narrow strip
of tread fifteen feet above me. Stifling a scream,
I talked her down, step by step, squeezed her so tightly
she yelped in pain. With friends, with family, she is
my sleeper—her full potential as yet unknown—
even to the Buddha who claims to know it all.

## Kraken

Keeping to herself, she derives no joy
from the social sea. Focused instead on
the work at hand, she moves giant, cupped
arms that pull and push the water, fanning
eggs to feed them oxygen. Her beak, tucked
into bubbled flesh, recalls the crack of clam
shells, the crunch of shark cartilage. Now
hunger hollows her, bulbs her eyes, pulls
at ringed flesh so thinned skin appears
translucent. She withers for months until
the octopi hatch and she can die. What
price this strength, this terrifying resolve?
It takes a hard-ass woman to raise her
young. Just ask any teenage girl.

## Je mange mes mots

Yes, it's cruel. An unseemly gluttony.
Trapping the ortolan buntings, forcing
them to gorge in the dark, mouthfeel of seeds
their only comfort in that closed, blank space.

Drowned in amber brandy, plucked then roasted,
their tiny bones crunch softly in the mouth.
The smallish wings tuck along smooth, browned skin,
like stiff Olympic lugers eaten whole.

A white cloth napkin drapes over the head
to hide the diner's shame from the sight of
God. If that were true, I'd buy them in bulk,
wash, dry, and press them, carry folded stacks

everywhere I went, place them as needed.
Once, I carried my girl child inside me
like a burden, her cabbage head pressing
on my softened cervix, an aching pain

so agonizing I wanted her out
at all costs. My brother said *there is no
home safer for her than your body.* I
want this to be untrue. My sweet girl, just

now a woman, is hustling tips from old,
rheumy-eyed men who tell her *smile real
pretty for me.* She is home, giving me
her day, and I am dishing out advice

like I have all the answers. When she's had
enough, she stomps up to her room, cocoons
herself in piled clothes and empty dishes.
Later, in the kitchen, I see she has

eaten what I left her: a simple green
salad, grilled chicken thigh lightly seasoned.
Instead, I should have said *I'm sorry*, should
have said *there's no mistake I haven't made.*

## Dirt Move

She calls it a "dirt move," my habit
of starting another conversation
when she's in the middle of hers.
It seems I can't pretend I'm interested
in the life of this twelve-year-old girl,
even one who's funny and bright and has
a big-toothed smile that slices my heart
at unexpected times. When she said it
I asked if she'd heard this from some clever
boy at school. *You think I'm not smart enough?*
she screamed, justly, and I knew she had me
dead to rights, that I fail her in ways better
mothers do not fail. When I'm returned
to dust, she will remember this.

## Stranger Things

Driving from North Carolina, we pull off
at a rest stop just outside of Charlottesville,
thirty miles from our new home. We're parked
on the truck side, away from the highway
so there'll be more grass for the dog.
Our daughter is in the car, tuned out
from the world and into her favorite Netflix
series. I'm in and out in minutes, wary
since I was thirteen when my father told me
what happened in a bathroom stall
to the wife of his fellow cop while he read
the paper in his car. I see the stranger talking
to my husband, and the body I know so well
tells me he's on guard. I move closer.
The man, small and snake-headed, is wearing
a jacket emblazoned with a Confederate flag.
His smile frames rotted teeth, and he is moving
closer to my husband who is taking care to keep
more distance between them. I say not a word,
slide into the passenger's seat, lock all the doors,
put my hand in the glovebox. Once, to help save
our marriage, I consented to my husband's need
to carry a gun, to feel like he could protect
his family. In this moment, I will do
whatever I can to protect this family.

# III

## End of Days

Honey, this shouldn't be hard.
You've been weighing
this question for months,
twisting over it. Just picture
the end of days, horses
of every color, white, fiery
red, black and the pale
one that Death straddles
with real pleasure. Now look how
the other riders drive them,
the sword-wielding lot
that won't scruple earthquakes,
blackened sun, the bloodied moon
like stains on your favorite
linen sheets. Look there—
the mountains and islands
forced from their original
foundations, those fat cats and
their no good brethren
smashed to pieces. It is
the rapture of the bride
upon you, the trumpet call
dragging you toward
oblivion. There remains
just this single question: whose
face do you see in those last
moments? The second
you walk through that cloudy
veil, whose hand are you
holding? No. Clawing.

## Menagerie of Broken Things

A handful of buttons, snapped
in half and chipped like teeth.
Shoelaces of every length
and color, some torn at one end.
The angel ornament, its missing
arm more visible now than
when it was attached. Wine
damaged books, torn t-shirts,
one pump with its heel
shorn off clean. This is not
to say I'll toss just any old
thing in among the others.
I carefully turn each one
over in my hand,
discerning its weakness,
its strength. Sometimes
I draw them all to me, press
them against my warm skin
and wonder what they'd be
without their particular
maladies: the obsessions,
the weed, without the Scotch.
I wonder what I'd be.

## Copulatory Embrace

All winter, females have waited on
the bottom of the bay while males
lounge on dirt floors of the estuaries.
Now they move from wintering

grounds to marsh-lined banks or beds
of submerged vegetation. A male
stands on the tips of walking legs,
waving and flexing his claws, fanning

pheromones toward the female crab
with his swimming paddles. He snaps
and kicks up sand, and, if seduced,
she edges toward him, turning

as she wedges under his body. He taps
and rubs her claws with sapphire tips
until she stills, folds her claws,
allows him to clasp and carry her

until ecdysis begins and her carapace
softens. As her abdomen rounds
from V to U and water fills the voids,
he spins her upside down,

clasps her tightly to his abdomen
Hinging to expose tiny gonopores,
she collects sprayed spermatophores
during their twelve-hour embrace.

After, he holds her just long enough
for her shell to harden. While this
mating will last her a lifetime, he will
cop his next embrace with equal vigor.

## Cooper's Rules

I. "All guns are loaded."

Except for this: as soon as you realize
that some guns are not, you let your guard down.
And before you know it, a loaded gun
slips into the mix and you find yourself
in real trouble. Say the gun is sexy
and shows some real talent. Maybe its lines
are smooth and the coldness of the metal
excites you, the danger stirs in you
a feeling you haven't had in quite some time.
You pick up that gun and feel its strange weight
in your hand, and now you can't put it down.

II. "Never let the muzzle cover anything you don't plan to destroy."

See, the thing with guns is that they're made
to do some kind of damage, inflict some
kind of hot pain, bore through soft tissue
or shatter bone. They're not made to comfort
anyone, to bring soup if you're sick
or make you feel better when you've had a bad day.
They won't remember how you like your steak
or why you don't like that Eagles song
that everyone else seems to love. Guns are
narcissists from sight to grip, and they
will never change. Don't turn the muzzle toward you.

III. "Keep your finger off the trigger 'til your sights are on the target."

For the love of all that is good and pure
do not put your finger on the trigger
of that gun you can't make yourself put down.

IV. "Identify your target and what is behind it."

And once you think you know what it is
you want, think again. Take a few steady breaths.
Look and see what's collateral before
you lift that gun and ease that trigger back.
Prepare for the kick and the boom. Don't cry.

## Drink Ghazal

Were my veins filled with Scotch instead of blood,
would you lift my wrist to lips, drink not-blood?

Liquor from my veins draws through thin pale skin.
Viscous, thick, held tight like hands is real blood.

It can be saved, can save a dying man,
pouring back life into a body, blood.

Unlike that bitter poison you tip back,
it does not change the marrow, this good blood.

Red, healthy living blood, real blood will not
make dry hot thirst for more and more not-blood.

Once your Lion leaves you, love, the trail will
no doubt show you where I've gone. Look for blood.

## Fallout

Following the light, their golden
faces are, by sundown, heavy
and low with cares. Still, I can't tear

myself away, not now. You'd say
do it, run from this bright hot porch,
this lovely field of sunflowers

mocking you with their likeness,
with their sacrifice. Mornings
they are young and fresh, their tiny

florets dripping dew while threaded
roots finger delta soil, seeking
copper and zinc, drawing them

up and into leaves and stalks.
They hold it all—mouths cupping
poisons unseen by the casual

observer. In Fukushima, scientists
planted fields of them, delighting
villagers until others came and cut

them down, toted away polluted
carcasses. You'd say I can't be
someone else's medicine.

Watch me.

## My Vampyre

*Who could resist his power? His tongue had dangers and toils to recount.*
    – John William Polidori, *The Vampyre*, 1819

His approach was so direct
I failed to sense the danger
I was in. Surrounded as
I was by good pens and hearts,
I took him for one who sees
the world the way I see it.
I beg you, Gentle Reader,
hear me out. While I am no
innocent, while I have seen
the world of men in all its
depravity, I was fooled.
Little did I suspect such
cunning, such skill in the art
of storytelling. His eyes
a lapis lazuli, his
shoulders broad, a rakish smile
dazzled me with the sharp heat
of what I ought to have known.
Reader, look away as I
wreck myself on the cold rocks
he has chosen for me.

## The Lost Boys, 1987

Facing the screen, he whispered
*you never see them fly,*
and it took me a little while
to know for sure he spoke a truth.
The camera hovered above
the earth, aimed at the ground they
came to claim. We never saw
their rootless feet, their flailing arms,
and missed the exact moment when
their pale, lithe bodies touched the plane
the rest of us inhabit, when
they seemed almost human.

I curled on the couch
between legs that gripped me tightly
until he let me go so he could pour *one*
*more*, then another, then *one more*.

You know how this movie ends.

## Familiar

In this fairytale cottage tucked into
an electric green mountain, circled by

snakes and every kind of biting thing,
she waits for him. The floors swept clean, cupboards

stocked with all that he loves, she clears spaces
for him to work, to heal. Her hands rub clean

the pimpled flesh of whole chickens in warm
running water, two wings like folded arms

of babes—slippery, delicate chest recalls
nighttime baths. She chops crone-knuckled ginger,

onions, a fistful of flat-leafed parsley
and drops them into steaming cauldrons slick

with dumplings. Slitting fat eye roasts, she stabs
them with garlic, baptizes with Chenin

Blanc. Squash she juliennes into lovely
legs. A sparkling brut sweats in a bucket

as she remakes the bed, folds hospital
corners, plumps the pillows, imagines his hands,

manly, cupping her breasts, caressing
her waist, then beckoning her to straddle him,

as he rocks her hips gently then not gently.
She counts out days ahead. Are there enough?

In this sort of fairytale there are no
demons, no cannibals, witches to aid.

There is only this familiar scene: a
woman setting right what is broken.

## Confession

A poet I admire, a good man, asked me
"Are you a nun?" We share an acquaintance,

a nun we both know. But on this morning
I laughed too loudly with an energy

I could not explain to this gentle man,
and when he turned to search my eyes with his,

I nearly told him everything: how I
couldn't eat, how the fluttering of this

unhappy bird in my chest caught my breath,
how you can believe so firmly you are

one person only to discover you're
someone else entirely. This fine man

might have found something to love in me still,
might have told me this is the world, we are

all sinners. For the dark gift that means I
can never love what I hold in my hands,

would he have asked God's forgiveness on my
behalf? I have had more lovers than friends.

## The Shopping

Sometimes it happens
in the grocery store
when, like my mother,
I am pressing
round, purple-brown
avocados to my lips to test their
ripeness. I spot
a woman, short with dark hair,
fresh-faced,
inhaling a bouquet
of cilantro. I think that's
the one who will
cook him healthy foods,
replacing Lean Cuisines
stacked in his freezer.
Or I'll be running my
steady pace through town,
where a pretty girl is
walking her smoke-coated
dog and coaxing her
so sweetly. I just know
she'll put up with his
silences, his need
to share his feelings
through touch, his
growling, drunken fits
of misanthropy.
At church I'll see
a freckled ginger
whose head is bent
in prayer, and I'll think
she's the one who'll
convince him, a man
who says he doesn't
need God, to consider

the alternative, to repent.
When friends ask
in some crowded bar
or quiet bookstore
who I'm looking for,
I say *no one*.

## Thigmotaxis

When we sleep, we are like children, moving
toward the body beside us or away.

An unconscious or fully knowing touch
draws us closer to its heat or pushes

us to the edge to explore cooler climes,
open fields. How simple it would be if

we were only one kind of animal
and found ourselves lying next to someone

who's like us on any given day. It's
come to this: I'm studying the quivering

throats of birds who warble from atop my
garden pagoda, their delicate, round

bodies filling with air, contracting with
freedom, not desire. I swear I never

used to be a woman who observes birds
so closely, cold and lovely though they be.

## Mutualism

The alga, the fungus embrace, lichen's
eager lovers, their lacy greens and whites
tumbling into playful patterns
entwined so tightly the naked eye
can't pull them apart.
Settling on rocks, on roots,
even on gravestones that support their
rough play, they seek every kind
of surface on which to spread
their gaudy love,
their obscene coupling.
This unlikely union brings one hope,
suggests others not heretofore considered
or even entertained.

## Steady, Girl

They say the best ones stay forever,
no matter how skittish, how wild-eyed
and restless their stall mates, the horses
they're meant to calm. Entering
the pen, the goats draw out
the twitching poison, work
quietly to free mile after mile
of glistening horsehide
from the hard tug of fear and longing,
the animal need to run in all directions
at once, to be nowhere and to be
everywhere in the world. See
the short gait that never matches
long strides, the strange rectangular
pupils, bright sideways slits
soothing these hot beasts
quivering with singular talents.

When she leaves you, remember
it's no one's fault. No love will
ever hold her, no devotion
will be nearly enough.

## Collateral

Let me begin by saying I love them all.
The tall girl with big shoulders two rows up,
her Adidas white and new. In the seat
behind me, the prattling boy whose mother
doubtless fears the pressure thumbing
his tiny eardrums, the pink, untested cochlea.
I love the pilot, whose words reveal the faintest
whiff of a boyhood in Virginia. For years
I've crossed myself before takeoff,
a trailing habit from Catholic school. Now I do it
purposefully, an act of love for every beating
heart whose life I risked by choosing my own
poisoned desires. When this plane goes down,
as I'm certain it will, save them, not me,
who was once beloved.

## Wreck and Ruin

What did you think would happen,
knowing what he is? You saw
the writing on that wonder
wall, bartering lines between
other lines, the haunted house
on fire, and ashes, always
ashes. He told you it's
so hard to be without you,
which made you love him.
But he was never clean was
he? My sweet Carolinas,
didn't our mothers teach us
better? No matter, we will
pick you up in your time of
need. He'll ask, do you still love
me? Say no. When doomsday comes
he won't be around. You will
shiver and shake, anything
he says now won't make sense.
Weren't we broken anyway?
On this tightrope, prisoners?
You say you're afraid, you see monsters.
You aren't safe when he's tired of
giving up. We just might save
you now, have you follow us
before he wrecks you like a
ball. Love, let go. Be lucky now.
Sweet illusions be damned.

## Retold

*"Orpheus,"* Eurydice cried, *"what madness has destroyed my
wretched self, and you?"*
   (Virgil, The Georgics)


Step carefully, friends. Follow close at my heels.
Trust me to hold back thorny stems that scratch shins,
lift low, eye-gouging branches, sidestep loose stones
and muddied holes threatening Dryad ankles.
Do be careful; use your hands if they help. Move
slowly over fallen trees, their twisted roots.

                 Let me show you what I've found in these dark woods.

Do you see these fired daylilies? Their velvet,
tangerine heads held up by long, strong necks? Note
the tiny, clenched fists of the mountain laurel,
the purple, swollen fingers of wild orchids,
water hopscotching rocks wherever the stream
bends. Hundreds of dollhouse ferns, electric green,
overgrow these paths, take back what men once claimed.

Up ahead, that man, my lover, will not wait,
will not stop to admire what I see. He won't,
I've learned, turn back for me. He will study trail
maps, look for painted markers tacked to live oaks,
repeat his stories—the same lyre notes I've heard
again and again. Watch him greet every wild
dog, insist that it love him, lick him with all
three tongues. Slick with self-interest, my lover stomps
on large feet (progress of the unencumbered).
Knowing my fears, primordial, unyielding,
he warned snakes coil in shadowed, cool places. To
some this seemed a kindness. I once thought so, too.

Why don't we linger here while he moves on? Soak

in the honest sun that shines on you, on me?
The god Hymen predicted failure. Friends, I
cannot say I wasn't warned.

## Run

For years I steered clear of the gravel
road that curves left by the spooky house
where turkey vultures regularly perch
along the roof's thin spine, waiting for
something to die. All my father's
careful lessons should stand the hairs
at attention on the back of my neck
as I run with a heavy exhale past
the falling down stone barn by the river,
the most remote place you can imagine.
I'm on my own here, and sinister shadows
mottle the road, Still I run until my
lungs and strong dark arms ache, until my
quadriceps swell with the effort
of pumping legs. I don't look
behind me, never scan the horizon
for dangers. No field of ticks, no rabid
dog, no controlling man threatens me.
I am well past being afraid, past
worrying that I won't return to
the ones I love, whole and in my right
mind. All the things I once feared now
rendered powerless in light of what
I've done, of what I've chosen to do.

**IV**

## Untenable

Looking down from my second story porch
I see the flowering quince they say will thrive
in almost any soil. This one is no
doubt dead, though its faithful branches reach up
and outward, insulting the brittle dry
sticks that pin the massive bush to fertile
ground. Watery red flowers the color
of diluted blood once bloomed in winter
on its bare and twisted branches, and in
springtime, the dark leaves bore small sharp teeth
so that I thought nothing in the natural world
could kill it. But who am I to make such
bold assumptions? Who knows for certain which
ones must be nurtured, how fragile love?

## Pilgrim

When you leave your home they will ask you why,
wonder at the strangeness of the act, think

the very worst. They will whisper words like
*bitter* or *heartbroken* or, worst of all,

*done*. When you finally come around, they'll
clap you on the back, ask you with their fixed

gaze *Are you sorry?* You won't answer with
the truth, you won't say no, you're not sorry,

you left because one bright day you opened
your eyes in your beautiful home, looked at

your growing children and your faithful, big-
eyed dog and knew you had to run, had to

leave the place where love shipwrecks you for a
lifetime, where every move you make is

insured by the ones you love. There is strength
in doing the hardest thing, in striking

out and settling on unfriendly shores. There
is strength, and on days when the rains roll in,

the skies darken and the air smells like peat,
there is sadness and maybe something more.

## Virginia Is for Lovers

    after Henri Cole


How long will it be
before I start feeling like
this place is our home?

Before the strange corners
squatting in this house
stop gouging my hips.

Before our neighbors
quit bringing us bread
and handwritten notes.

Will my new license plate
always taunt me with its
prescription for love?

Everyone says to give it
time, as though time were
the sandy bits of kibble

I drop at the dog's feet
when he's been a good boy.
No matter how much I give him,

he never mistakes these gestures
for his supper. Whining at his bowl,
he urges me to follow

trodden paths, to acknowledge
then, disregard anomalies
of action and reward.

When do I stop holding
everything I love
like it's broken?

## Homecoming

Each time I return to this house that doesn't
feel like my house, I enter like a thief or
a victim. Pushing on the door I listen
for alien sounds that whisper *turn and run*
to wherever you've come from, wherever you've
been. Its tidy, hushed dignity does not stop
me from opening closets on the second
floor or dropping down to my hands and knees to
view the space below each bed. I test the glass
knob on the attic door, look for the folded
paper I've stuffed into its crack—proof the house
has not betrayed me. The potted plants eye me
with limp need as I practice these rituals.
Patient as an empty chair, this house shows
no signs it's had enough. Gently sighing,
it reckons that the years will pass and one day
I'll come home and forget to check the locks.

## Welcome Home

I'm getting used to feeling exposed by the curtain-less
windows. I like the idea of someone watching me
through them from the other side of the street,
or maybe from next door. I wander from room
to room, naked and listening to the strange sounds
this house makes. The spooky whir of the washer,
the way one plank in the bedroom makes the
attic door rattle like someone's trying to get out
or in. The nails won't stop poking up from the floor,
tearing at my soles. Now I'm squatting on the bed
with my hair hanging down around my face,
embracing every fear as it comes to me,
too tired to shuffle them into orderly rows.
I wonder when the neighbors will start complaining.

# Hemlock

"Killers," says my friend, holding the branch delicately
between two fingers, gesturing to the fuzzy white beads
clinging to the needles of the Eastern hemlock tree he's

pulled it from. I know nothing of trees, of the insects
that devour them with sucker mouths—*wooly adelgids*—
he calls them, his lovely drawl pulling at the vowels.

These days we leave our homes for exercise and food,
the reason I'm straddling a knobby-tired bike at the base
of a Virginia mountain. I ask with interest if this is Socrates'

hemlock, and like a tired professor used to silly questions,
he tells me no, I've confused it for the plant with leaves
like parsley, the one animals eat then return to even as it's

strangling them. Suddenly, on this remote gravel road
where we've stopped to honor the dying, an ugly, bow-legged
man with a MAGA cap appears, scuttles up to us and extends

his hand. I recoil, and he thinks it's the distancing, but my
friend keeps him talking while I walk my bike back, watch
his movements closely like my father taught me. The man

is powerfully built beneath a dirty t-shirt and jeans. His head
shaved bald, it is impossible to know how old he is: sixty five?
He looks me over slowly, toes to top, a question forming

on his face. Now he's talking about "the Chinese virus,"
of bears and rattlesnakes in May. "Never know what all
you'll find along this road," he says, and I think *how true*.

Picturing the church-turned-house we passed two miles
back, a large Confederate flag nearly concealing the scrolled
crosses on its front doors, I am convinced this man lives

there, though I have no evidence this is true. Eventually
he moves on, and I exhale, relaxing the muscles in my gut.
We pedal in silence, his words threatening to poison

this cloudless day. After a while I turn to my friend
and ask him to tell me again about the *wooly adelgids*,
how people come from everywhere to save the trees.

## Ghost Trees (Albino Redwoods)

The heartless, the myopic call us vampires,
parasites, though we are neither of these.
It is true we cannot feed ourselves, cannot
make our food from light alone, we need the others.
Large stomata in our leaves, an anomaly, send
water into the air—an endless crying jag. Our
roots feed from the ground, absorb all the metals,
all the poisons. Yes, we've been ridiculed, we've
been doubted and blamed. And if you spot us
shimmering incandescent in the canopy, you'll
think us a trick of light, an impossibility. We
are rare, and docents hide us to keep us safe.
Unlike animals, we cannot run. We are poets,
and we are sometimes loved to death.

## That House

Think of the energy we put into that house. Scrubbing its sinks,
vacuuming the headsful of hair that gathered in every corner
like tumbleweeds. Consider the coats of brights and neutrals you
brushed onto every wall, the doorstoppers and screens you replaced,
the bookcases we assembled until our thumbs ached. Think of the
floor pocks we grieved over after that dinner party where someone's
warn heel exposed a nail. Those windows that needed washing haunt
my early waking hours, as does the length of the grass that you
nurtured and cut, year after year. The red bud that we raised from a
stick is coming along, sure to bloom any year now, rewarding
someone else with the blood red petals I've seen already in my mind.
To think I picked up and started again in some other place with
people I don't know. It's not the effort that discourages me, not the
friends and family I left behind. I'm ashamed to tell you that it's that
house, the thought of other people breathing and sleeping inside its
walls. I want to believe that a house cares who's dusting its broad,
lovely banisters, who's worrying over its drafts.

## The House Speaks

There was a time when we were happiest on our own.
From the moment the sun caressed the faux wooden slats
of the blinds and she stretched, arms overhead, to
the moment in bed when her book tipped onto her chest,
signaling it was time to put her glasses on the table
and flick off the light. The lavender smells of her showering
and the soft squeaks as she wiped the bathroom mirror made
me smile. Attending to whatever it is that kept her from me
all day long, I was patient, still. But once she came through our
side door and put down her bag and books, hung up her keys
and pulled her shoes off, placing them carefully into their slot
on the hanging rack behind the door, she was mine. We chopped
vegetables for curry, drank a glass of white wine, ate slowly
and washed up. Evenings she'd curl on the couch to watch
our favorite shows. Don't tell me we weren't happy.

## Land of the Lotus Eaters

It's not the oppressive artificial fruits
everywhere in bowls, or the oversized bags

of pistachios stuffed into the corners,
or the bottles of pills that crowd their kitchen

counters. The television screams its usual
pitch, and they are nodding at me, telling me

stories they have told a dozen times or more,
smiling, pinning me in place like Odysseus's

men eating petals from the warm, indolent
hands of their captors. On the phone, my bright boy

asks if my parents have loved me enough, if
I'm ready to come home. He's joking, but I say

I am drowning. I say, I must get out.
I say I can never leave this place again.

## Johns Hopkins Hospital, at the Corner of Orleans and N. Broadway

In the car, you take a deep breath. You're leaving
her here, drains protruding from her jaw and thigh,
dried blood caking her tongue, eyes following you
to the door. You're headed home where you'll fall
into bed and sleep the stunned sleep of dread
and heartache. At the corner of Orleans and North
Broadway, a girl steps in front of your headlights
like she's walked onto a stage, her greasy blond hair
framing the good bones in her face and the eyes
glistening with opioid light. She is dirty, but the track
pants and t-shirt look like they were once clean,
once worn by the redhead you teach who always
rolls out of bed and into her chair five minutes
late every day, clean hair pulled back into a top-knot,
sleep crumbs still gathered at the corners of her
green eyes. Because you're slower than usual,
because you've spent these last days folded
into waiting room chairs, making good news
out of bad and listening to the private tragedies
of strangers, you don't look away in time to avoid
the gaze, the darkened teeth, the slight frame
that has been violated in ways too gruesome
to fathom. The red light is endless. You rest
your forehead on the steering wheel for you don't
know how long until you hear a soft tapping on
your window, and the girl is pointing to the light
that's now green, and you drive on.

## Something

They said, take something of hers, something soft.
I couldn't. Everything I thought to take
was too painful to bear away from that house.
But here you are—her blanket hefted in
my child's thin arms—now settled on my couch.
During the daylight hours the dog burrows
deep in your folds, and each night, cocooning
herself inside your heaviness, my girl
trails her fingers along your edges, sniffs
for a certain perfume she hopes you've trapped.
I take slow, deep swigs from the Maker's Mark,
eye you, suspicious from my corner post.
Egyptians once buried their dead with all
their goods. Gladly I'd have placed the last stone.

## The Trees

*Sometimes they cry*, he says, staring
out the bay window. At first I think
he means my brother and me, that
he's talking to our dead mother,
gone for seven months. But he
only speaks to her in low mutterings,
the volume of intimacy and habit.
He's talking to me about the river
birch he planted right before
she got sick again. He hated
their peeling skins, a nuisance
when he mowed. *I asked Tyler*,
he says, naming the lawn guy
I've never met who knows my father
better these days than I do. I picture
the two of them nodding at mulch,
shaking their heads at grubs. *When
it gets hot, they take up water they
don't need, cry it out.* I let this sink in,
eye the stiff, cracking birch bark my
mother loved, the darkened trunks
a reminder of slow dying.
I lift my glass to the trees, nod
in their direction. I say *good for them.*

## My Mother's Kitchen

Spinning and spinning around her cluttered
kitchen, reaching for the sesame oil
in its stained metal canister, for black
bean paste, the *gochujang* she kept in big
plastic tubs in the frig in the garage,
I do my best with rushed dishes, shortcut
substitutes for the meals my mother made.
My daughter, a state away and still a
teenager, would have made fine work of it.
For years she shadowed my mother in her
kitchen, absorbing every word without
rancor or defensiveness, without stoned
silence or the impatience I showed at
her age and well beyond it. I can see
my girl, pigeon toed at the stove, stirring
*dubu jigae* with a large wooden spoon,
her hand balanced on her hip, fingers tapping.
Why is it hard to love each other?

## Third Sunday

*Touch me and see, because a ghost does not have flesh and bones*
*as you can see I have.*
  – Luke 24

As I settle into the pew next to my daughter
they appear—mother, father, two small children drawing,
filling in the lines with colored pencils, their dark heads
bent in concentration. At the end of the row,

the grandmother sits, and suddenly I'm thankful
I am wearing my good black pants and carrying a decent
bag instead of clutching my keys or shoving them deep
into pockets of torn jeans. She is not my mother,

though everything about her suggests she could be.
The unmistakable heft of her dark hair, a soft
scarf tied around her thin, pale neck, the dark clothes
that look like they were bought in Busan or Seoul.

I watch her closely, see how she corrects each child
with a look, her hand on a small head. I look down
at my shoes. They could use a polish, just like my nails,
bitten, jagged. I hear her voice in my head, hissing

*uk-keh*, and I stand up straighter, draw my shoulders back.
Just then I notice tears slipping down my girl's cheek,
her shoulders shaking. She sees her, too, and so I reach
for her small living hand, press my palm to hers.

## Once, I Thought He Knew Everything

I find my father's stash of magazines stacked neatly
in a bathroom drawer. Thumbing through them,
I scan the articles I know he pours over: liberal
conspirators, women who carry firearms, home
invaders stopped dead by "armed citizens."
I realize he's quit telling me these stories,
that the magazines no longer appear on his dining
room table, that he's prepared for my visit.
Later, I watch him as he fills the tractor tires
with air, kneeling by each one, pressing down
to feel the give. No gauge to guide his work,
he does it all by touch, by instinct and experience.
It's been years since I've watched him work,
squatted by him while he changed the oil in the car,
since I happily fetched him a tool or tilted the light
for him to see. His long sleeves rolled to the elbow,
glasses perched on the end of his nose, he narrates
his movements, convinced that one day I'll need
this information, that I'll be pumping up tires when
I'm not at my keyboard or sipping green tea lattes
at Starbucks. His hands, creased and spotted now,
are still more than competent, more than capable.
Once, I thought he knew everything.

## Inherited

Knowing me as he does, he steels himself for a volley of tiresome questions, each one more condescending, more impatient than the last. By the time his doctor opens the door, I'm throbbing with anxiety disguised as anger, a trick I learned from this wheezing, wasted man. Seeing him here, quietly submitting, I remember climbing out my bedroom window at seventeen. Catching my shirttail on the jutting bricks below the sash, I fell four feet into the rhododendron and bloodied my back. He said nothing as he swabbed my cuts with peroxide and bandaged them, offering me two aspirins and the solace of silence, the chance to forget my humiliation. After checking his pulse and tapping on his back, listening intently with his instruments, the thirty-something doctor asks my father his own condescending questions too quietly for the old man's ears. *What did he say?* my father asks later, flinching already at the words he expects to hear. *He says you're doing fine*, I respond.

## Filial

Never mind that I am here for him,
that I've returned to this house I swore

I would never sleep in again.
He is crumbling. The stiff bricks of his

body, once pointed and strong, need
tending, as does this house, the broken

banister and chipped paint signaling
decline. Never mind that now I

make the rules, that I decide what
we're eating, when we're leaving, what

pills we take with what, who we trust, who
we don't trust. My father hangs

on my every word, wags his
head at me like Gogol's plaster

cat, obediently heads off
to bed hours before I climb into

mine, exhausted and numb. I sleep
dreamless in my father's house,

my brain emptied of all its troubles,
The ancient slights and disappointments

of the once beloved, then maligned,
I sleep like I never sleep in my

bright and book-lined home,
brimming with the busy lives of

my children. In my father's house,
buried in the detritus of

an old life, I'm mortared, safe
and unsafe, sound and collapsing.

## Grief Cat

Circling the edges of these rooms,
he rubs the sides of his belly,
his fisted face on every vertical
plane—each wall and table leg,
each stair spindle—pretending
not to see me. Just when I forget
to look for him, when the folds
of my brain are fat with work
or I think I'm too tired to dream,
grief cat pounces from an unseen
height or springs from a space too
small to hold him. At the bottom
of my closet he finds the shoes
I bought her, the ones I took back.
Curling heavy on my chest while
I'm sleeping, grief cat watches
me stare into this mirror, see
the curves of her face and lines
burrowing deeper. Stretching long
on the couch, flicking his tail,
he studies me with dark orbs
that see all I've lost. Relentless,
shifty, if he moves I'll never
see him coming.

## Big Pipe Creek

On days when the rains swelled the creek
it hardly seemed a creek, its raw
muddy edges climbing quickly,
bearlike up the banks, dragging
sticks and snakes and god knows what all
to the untrimmed fields that framed my
grandfather's house. As a child, I feared
those rains that sometimes closed
the road, forced my father to backtrack
until we turned on the higher path
that led to the house from the other
side. Once my grandfather abandoned
the house, moved up the hill to the brick
bungalow he went about neglecting,
too, I would drive onto the overgrown
property by the creek, alone.
Every five years or so, some
reckless boy would venture out
into the creek during a storm
and drown in its swirling violence,
his white shoulders washed onto
the shore miles downstream. I never
imagined that I'd build a house
near that creek, watch hawklike as my
baby girl ran laughing along its tall
slopes, warn my teenage son
about the swelling waters and
hairpin curve that fooled even
seasoned drivers, pushing them
against the guardrail and over
the edge of the bridge into a
dark wall of water. One day
I gathered up the courage to leave
that place where the bend and the creek

commune, where just about all of
what I know turned out to be wrong.

# Notes

Information on the Jeju Folklore and Natural History Museum can be found here:
https://www.visitjeju.net/en/detail/view?contentsid=-CONT_000000000500545#

Jeff Cooper (1920-2006) popularized the use of the handgun for personal protection and then offered safety advice for guns.

In 2019 the *New York Times* reported that singer-songwriter Ryan Adams was accused of sexual harassment and exploitation by, among others, his ex-wife Mandy Moore. My poem, "Wreck and Ruin," uses titles and lyrics from his songs.

# Acknowledgments

The following journals published many of these poems, some in earlier versions and with different titles:

*Able Muse*: "My Mother's Kitchen"
*American Journal of Poetry*: "Cooper's Rules"
*Arkansas International*: "Confession"
*Atlanta Review*: "I stop somewhere waiting for you"
*The Boiler*: "Homecoming"
*Birmingham Poetry Review*: "Fallout," "Menagerie of Broken Things," "Ride Along," and "The Shopping"
*Blackbird*: "Guarding George Wallace"
*Cherry Tree*: "Filial"
*Chicago Quarterly Review*: "The House Speaks"
*The Cortland Review*: "End of Days" and "Steady, Girl"
*Crab Orchard Review*: "Doll's House, Provincetown Museum"
*Cutleaf Journal*: "Scorpling" and "Familiar"
*december magazine*: "Elegy for Farmer Pak," "Big Pipe Creek," "Land of the Lotus Eaters," and "Pilgrim"
*Fifth Wednesday Journal*: "Once, I Thought He Knew Everything"
*Fledgling Rag*: "Copulatory Embrace"
*Four Way Review*: "Untenable"
*Free State Review*: "Sokcho, South Korea"
*The Good Men Project*: "Sometimes they come back to me in dreams"
*Hobart*: "Stone Grandfather"
*Ilanot Review*: "Reckless" and "Sleeper"
*Little Patuxent Review*: "Virginia is for Lovers"
*The Louisville Review*: "Doubles"
*Muse/A*: "Welcome Home"
*The Normal School*: "Dirt Move"
*Orion*: "Sting"
*Pangyrus*: "Noctambulist"
*The Pinch*: "Spondylosis"
*Prairie Schooner*: "Grief Cat"
*Prelude*: "Sun and Moon"
*Quiddity*: "That House"

*Redivider*: "My Father's Lessons"
*Reed Magazine*: "Ivy in the House"
*Rhino Poetry*: "Korean Wedding Ducks"
*The Rumpus*: "Wreck and Ruin"
*San Diego Poetry Annual*: "Johns Hopkins Hospital at the Corner of Orleans and N. Broadway"
*Seneca Review*: "Collateral"
*Shenandoah*: "Ghost Trees" and "Something"
*Southeast Review*: "The Bamboo Wife"
*The Southern Review*: "Dilettante" and "Retold"
*Spillway*: "Run"
*Sugar House Review*: "Hapa"
*The Sun*: "Je mange mes mots"
*Water-Stone Review*: "Kraken"

"Blind" appears in the anthology *This is What America Looks Like* (Washington Writers' Publishing House, 2021).

"The Heifer" won the Morton Marcus 2020 Poetry Award and was published in *phren-Z*.

"Pedal" and "Thigmotaxis" appear in *The Southern Poetry Anthology* (Texas Review Press, 2022).

## Gratitude

Thank you Kris Bigalk, Natasha Kane, and the team at Trio House Press for championing my work.

I'm grateful to the conferences and residencies that gave me direction and time, and I am especially thankful for the dear friends I made at the Fine Arts Work Center, The Hambidge Center, Longleaf Writers Conference, Sewanee Writers' Conference, and the Virginia Center for Creative Arts.

For the relentless faith they've shown in the words and in me, I am indebted to Lauren Alleyne, Matt Bondurant, Adam Latham, Seth Tucker, Adam Vines, and Snowden Wright.

Thanks to the workshop leaders and editors whose good hands are all over this thing: Nickole Brown, Jan Freeman, Ada Limón, Tom Lombardo, Charles Martin, Mary Jo Salter, Alicia Stallings, and Brian Turner.

For always being on my side (even when my side was obstructed), I am grateful to David Bushman, Grant and Elijah Disharoon, Christine McCauslin, Lynn and Tony Rosas, James Sevick (senior and junior), "The Gang" at Bridgewater College, and my students.

And finally, to my mother, Chong Mi Sok, whose voice will always be in my head—*gomawoyo eomeoni*.

## About the Author

Leona Sevick is the winner of the Press 53 Award for Poetry for her first full-length book of poems, *Lion Brothers*. Her work appears in *Orion*, *Birmingham Poetry Review*, *Blackbird*, *The Southern Review*, and *The Sun*. She was a 2019 Walter E. Dakin Fellow and 2018 Tennessee Williams Scholar for the Sewanee Writers' Conference, and she serves as an advisory board member of the Furious Flower Black Poetry Center at James Madison University. She is provost and professor of English at Bridgewater College in Virginia, where she teaches Asian American literature. *The Bamboo Wife* is her second full-length collection of poems.

# ABOUT THE BOOK

*The Bamboo Wife* was designed at Trio House Press through the collaboration of:

Natasha Kane, Lead Editor and Interior Design
Ali Shafer Supporting Editor
Joel W. Coggins, Cover Design

The text is set in Adobe Caslon Pro.

# ABOUT THE PRESS

**Trio House Press** is an independent literary press dedicated to discovering, publishing, and promoting books that enhance culture and the human experience. Trio House Press adheres to and supports all ethical standards and guidelines outlined by the CLMP. For further information, or to consider making a donation to Trio House Press, visit us online at triohousepress.org.

Printed in the USA
CPSIA information can be obtained
at www.ICGtesting.com
JSHW080552140624
64710JS00004B/112